JOHN F. KENNEDY

PIVOTAL PRESIDENTS
PROFILES IN LEADERSHIP

JOHN F.
KENNEDY

Edited by Sherman Hollar

Britannica®

Educational Publishing

IN ASSOCIATION WITH

ROSEN

EDUCATIONAL SERVICES

Published in 2013 by Britannica Educational Publishing
(a trademark of Encyclopædia Britannica, Inc.) in association with Rosen Educational Services, LLC
29 East 21st Street, New York, NY 10010.

Distributed exclusively by Rosen Educational Services.
For a listing of additional Britannica Educational Publishing titles, call toll free (800) 237-9932.

First Edition

Britannica Educational Publishing
J.E. Luebering: Director, Core Reference Group, Encyclopædia Britannica
Adam Augustyn: Assistant Manager, Encyclopædia Britannica

Anthony L. Green: Editor, Compton's by Britannica
Michael Anderson: Senior Editor, Compton's by Britannica
Andrea R. Field: Senior Editor, Compton's by Britannica
Sherman Hollar: Senior Editor, Compton's by Britannica

Marilyn L. Barton: Senior Coordinator, Production Control
Steven Bosco: Director, Editorial Technologies
Lisa S. Braucher: Senior Producer and Data Editor
Yvette Charboneau: Senior Copy Editor
Kathy Nakamura: Manager, Media Acquisition

Rosen Educational Services
Hope Lourie Killcoyne: Executive Editor
Nelson Sá: Art Director
Cindy Reiman: Photography Manager
Karen Huang: Photo Researcher
Brian Garvey: Designer, Cover Design
Introduction by Hope Lourie Killcoyne

Library of Congress Cataloging-in-Publication Data

John F. Kennedy/edited by Sherman Hollar.
    p. cm. — (Pivotal presidents: profiles in leadership)
"In association with Britannica Educational Publishing, Rosen Educational Services."
Includes bibliographical references and index.
ISBN 978-1-61530-943-6 (library binding)
1. Kennedy, John F. (John Fitzgerald), 1917-1963 — Juvenile literature. 2. Presidents — United States —
Biography — Juvenile literature. I. Hollar, Sherman.
E842.Z9J64 2013
973.922092 — dc23
[B]

2012022265

Manufactured in the United States of America

On the cover, p. 3: Behind the portrait of John F. Kennedy, 35th president of the United States, a
United States Navy ship is seen intercepting a Soviet ship in Cuban waters during the U.S. Naval blockade on that Soviet-backed country during the Cuban Missile Crisis, October, 1962. Kennedy was able to
avert nuclear disaster by means of both the blockade and tense but ultimately fruitful negotiations with
Soviet leader Nikita Khrushchev. *Carl Mydans/Time & Life Pictures/Getty Images*

Cover, p. 3 (portrait) John F. Kennedy Presidential Library and Museum; cover, pp. 1, 3 (flag) © iStock-
photo.com/spxChrome; pp. 5, 10, 22, 34, 52, 70, 73, 76, 78 Federov Oleksiy/Shutterstock.com

Table of Contents

INTRODUCTION

John F. Kennedy, c. *1961*. Library of Congress/Archive Photos/ Getty Images

On Sept. 26, 1960, John Fitzgerald Kennedy and Richard Milhous Nixon faced off in the first of an unprecedented series of four televised debates between two U.S. presidential nominees. It was a paradigm shift for the nation, the first time that Americans could see would-be leaders of the free world speaking at length, answering difficult questions, and doing so in a somewhat impromptu style. It allowed viewers—and there were 70 million of them that first night—to get a gut feeling about the two candidates. How do they think? How do they react under pressure? Do they smile? Grimace? Pause? Stall? Of course, television is a visual medium, and as JFK was younger, more charismatic, and better looking than his opponent (Nixon also had stubble and perspiration on his face), having the debates televised worked to JFK's advantage. Interestingly, many of those who heard the debates on radio rather than saw them believed that Nixon had won; the opposite was true for TV viewers. Did the visual dimension of television add the element of the superficial? Perhaps. But it was nonetheless a point of no return, redefining the process by which Americans choose their presidents.

Today, it is interesting to think about how the 35th president of the United States is remembered. Many Americans, old and young, can conjure up images of Kennedy, his equally photogenic wife, Jackie, and their two children, John and Caroline. Many can also hear some of JFK's famous lines, particularly, "Ask not what your country can do for you—ask what you can do for your country," complete with that distinctive Massachusetts/ Kennedy twang. It is also widely known that Kennedy was the youngest president ever elected. And the first Roman Catholic. But what many may not remember or even know in the first place is that before going into politics, he worked as a newspaper journalist, first at the *Chicago Herald American* and then at the International News Service. In addition, he wrote several books before becoming president, one of which was a best seller and another of which garnered a Pulitzer Prize.

What many also may remember about John F. Kennedy is how he died. Images of the Kennedys in that long black limousine in Dallas, Tex., were beamed live into television sets across America, and then repeatedly afterward. The shock of Kennedy's assassination was followed by the heartbreaking visual of his young son John Jr.—whose third birthday it was on the day of Kennedy's funeral—saluting as his father was buried.

But Americans were left not just with sorrow, but also with hope. Hope that following JFK's exhortations, the space race would be won. And that through programs such as the Peace Corps, which he established, Americans would indeed not just ask what they could do for their country, but for the world.

Pivotal Presidents: John F. Kennedy profiles the life of a leader whose mystique lives on, adding detail to the challenges and successes of Kennedy's time in office—as well as taking readers through his private life and early years. This book explores, examines, and explains the indelible moments and international crises of America's first extensively televised presidency.

CHAPTER 1

Early Life and Career

In November 1960, at the age of 43, John F. Kennedy became the youngest man ever elected president of the United States. (Theodore Roosevelt had become president at 42 when President William McKinley was assassinated, but he was not elected at that age.) On Nov. 22, 1963, Kennedy was shot to death in Dallas, Tex., the fourth United States president to die by an assassin's bullet.

Kennedy was the nation's first Roman Catholic president. He was inaugurated in January 1961, succeeding Republican President Dwight D. Eisenhower. In one of the closest elections in the nation's history, Kennedy had defeated the Republican candidate, Vice-President Richard M. Nixon, by little more than 100,000 votes. During

John F. Kennedy being sworn in as U.S. president, Jan. 20, 1961. Encyclopædia Britannica, Inc.

his time in office, Kennedy faced a number of foreign crises, especially in Cuba and Berlin, but managed to secure several landmark achievements, such as concluding the Nuclear Test-Ban Treaty with the Soviet Union and the United Kingdom, winning approval of the international economic development program Alliance for Progress, and creating a volunteer service, the Peace Corps, to help other countries in their development efforts.

THE KENNEDY FAMILY

President Kennedy's great-grandparents immigrated to the United States from Ireland in 1858. They settled in Boston, Mass. His grandfathers, Patrick J. Kennedy and John F. (Honey Fitz) Fitzgerald, were born there. Both men became influential in state politics. Honey Fitz served several terms as Boston's mayor and as a member of the United States House of Representatives. Patrick Kennedy was the powerful boss of a Boston political ward and served in both houses of the Massachusetts legislature.

Patrick's son, Joseph, was a brilliant mathematician. At the age of 25 he became the youngest bank president in the United States. His fortune continued to grow, and he was one of the few financiers to sense beforehand the stock market crash of 1929. He made hundreds of millions of dollars.

Joseph married Rose Fitzgerald, daughter of Honey Fitz, on Oct. 7, 1914. Their first child, Joseph, Jr., was born in 1915. John was born on May 29, 1917. Seven other children followed: Rosemary, Kathleen, Eunice, Patricia, Robert, Jean, and Edward (called Teddy). All were born in Brookline, Mass., a suburb of Boston.

A young John F. Kennedy dressed in a police officer costume. Encyclopædia Britannica, Inc.

EDUCATION AND ATHLETICS

Joseph Kennedy, Sr., set up a million-dollar trust fund for each of his children. This freed them from future financial worry and allowed them to devote their lives to public service, if they desired. As the children grew, their parents stressed the importance of competitive spirit. One of their father's favorite mottoes was: "Second place is a loser." The drive to win was deeply ingrained in the children, and they never did anything halfheartedly.

Kennedy family photo c. 1931: (left to right) Rosemary; Joseph, Jr.; Kathleen; Patricia; Rose; Joseph, Sr.; Jean; Eunice; John; Robert. Encyclopædia Britannica, Inc.

Their parents were careful to neglect neither the intellectual nor the physical development of the children. As they grew older, the children would eat their evening meals in two groups, divided by age. Mr. and Mrs. Kennedy ate at both meals. This allowed them to discuss subjects that were of interest to each group. All the children attended dancing school while very young, and all, with the exception of Rosemary, who did not take part in rough-and-tumble play, loved sports activities. The other children, however, thrived on

John F. Kennedy (seated, front row, far right) *photographed with the Dexter School football team.* Encyclopædia Britannica, Inc.

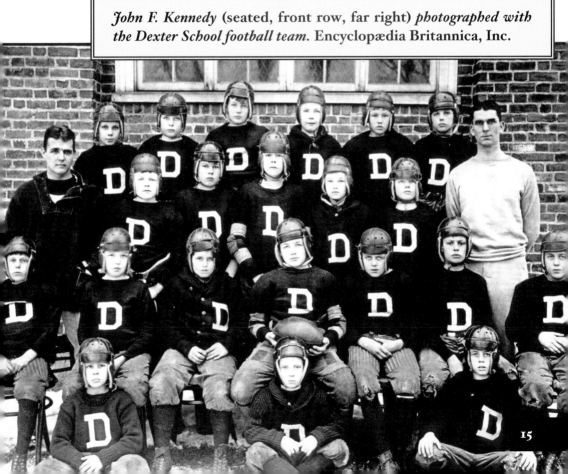

roughhousing. Even when they were adults, one of their favorite pastimes was a rousing and often bruising game of touch football.

On pleasant days, Mrs. Kennedy took her children for long walks. She made a point of taking them into church for a visit each day. "I wanted them to form a habit of making God and religion a daily part of their lives," she said later in life.

With this background, it was quite natural for John Kennedy and his brothers and sisters to excel in school and in sports. John attended public schools in Brookline. Later he entered private schools in Riverdale, N.Y., and Wallingford, Conn. In 1935 and 1936 he studied at the London School of Economics. Then he followed his older brother, Joe, into Harvard University. An excellent athlete, John was a star swimmer and a good golfer. His athletic activities, however, were cut down after he suffered a back injury in a Harvard football game. The injury was to plague him later in life.

John and his older brother were very close. While a young boy, Joe said that someday he would be president of the United States. The family took him at his word. Of all the children, Joe seemed the one most likely to enter the political field.

Joseph, Sr., was named ambassador to the United Kingdom in 1937. John and his older brother then worked as international reporters for their father. John spent his summers in England and much of the rest of his time at Harvard. The brothers often traveled to distant parts of the world to observe events of international importance for their father. The clouds of World War II were hovering over Europe at that time.

RETURN TO THE UNITED STATES AND COLLEGE

The senior Kennedy was a controversial ambassador. His candid remarks about the progress of the war in Europe earned him the disfavor of the English and of some of his countrymen in the United States. His family returned home in 1939, and he followed the next year.

John finished his studies at Harvard and graduated with honors in 1940. Later that same year he did graduate work in economics at Stanford University in California. He also expanded a college thesis into a full-length book entitled *Why England Slept*. It dealt with England's unpreparedness for World

War II and was based on John's own experiences while working for his father. The book became a best seller.

NAVAL SERVICE IN WORLD WAR II

A few months before the Japanese attacked Pearl Harbor in December 1941, John attempted to enlist in the United States Army. His old back injury kept him from being accepted. After several months of exercise, however, he was granted a commission in the Navy. Eventually he saw extensive action in the South Pacific and on one occasion barely escaped death in battle. Commanding a patrol torpedo (PT) boat, he was injured when a Japanese destroyer sank it in the Solomon Islands. Marooned far behind enemy lines, he led his men back to safety.

Nearly one year after John's narrow escape, Joe, Jr., a Navy pilot, was killed when his plane exploded in the air over the English coast. To his brother's memory, John wrote *As We Remember Joe*, a collection of tributes. In 1948 John's sister Kathleen died in an airplane crash in the south of France. She was the widow of the

John F. Kennedy sitting next to his brother Joseph Kennedy, Jr.,
both in naval uniforms, c. 1945. **Hulton Archive/Archive Photos/**
Getty Images

marquess of Hartington of England. He, too, had been killed in action during World War II, while leading an infantry charge in Normandy, France.

The Commander of *PT 109*

In August 1943, during a night action in the Solomon Islands, Kennedy's torpedo boat, *PT 109*, was rammed and cut in half by a Japanese destroyer. The force of the collision threw him to the deck, reinjuring his back. Despite

John F. Kennedy commanding the U.S. Navy torpedo boat PT 109, 1943. Encyclopædia Britannica, Inc.

this, he gathered the ten members of his crew together. One of the crew members was so badly injured that he was unable to swim. He was put into a life jacket. Kennedy gripped one of the jacket's straps between his teeth and towed the man as the crew swam to a nearby island. It took them five hours to reach it. For his heroism, Kennedy was awarded the Navy and Marine Corps medal, the Purple Heart, and a citation. (These events were later depicted in a Hollywood film, *PT 109* [1963], that contributed to the Kennedy mystique.) The back injury, however, put him out of action for the remainder of the war.

CHAPTER 2

Political Rise

The death of his brother deeply affected John F. Kennedy. Before the war, Joe had decided to carry on with his ambition to enter the political field. This decision caused a certain degree of disappointment for John because he, too, had considered pursuing a career in that field. He felt, however, that one Kennedy in politics was enough, and so John was determined to become a newspaperman. After his discharge from the U.S. Navy he worked for a short time as a correspondent for the *Chicago Herald American* newspaper and the International News Service. In 1946 he decided to enter the field of politics. To the Kennedy family, this was the most natural thing for John to do.

ELECTION TO CONGRESS

For his first target, Kennedy chose to try for a seat in the United States House of Representatives. He would represent the 11th Massachusetts Congressional District (a now-obsolete district in eastern Massachusetts). His family rallied to his side as he began his campaign for the nomination. Because the 11th District was predominantly Democratic, the candidate for the office would have no trouble being elected once he had gained the nomination. Kennedy and his family worked tirelessly. Their efforts, Kennedy's own impressive war record, and his family's political background greatly aided his campaign. He easily defeated eight other candidates running for the same nomination.

In office, Kennedy quickly established himself as a moderately independent thinker. Occasionally he voted against proposed measures that had met with the approval of his own Democratic Party. He was reelected in 1948 and 1950. An accomplished orator, the young congressman became a popular speaker.

His back injury, however, continued to bother him. He often appeared on the House floor and at speaking engagements supported by crutches. In 1946 he was named by the United States Chamber of Commerce as one of the nation's outstanding men of the year.

UNITED STATES SENATOR

In 1952 Kennedy decided to run for the United States Senate. His opponent was Republican senator Henry Cabot Lodge, Jr. Again the Kennedy family worked to get John elected. Kennedy defeated Lodge by more than 70,000 votes. The victory was particularly impressive because across the rest of the nation, Republican candidates were swept into office along with the landslide of votes for the new Republican president, Dwight D. Eisenhower.

In the Senate Kennedy had woolen textile tariffs raised and urged President Eisenhower to obtain an agreement with Japan to cut textile imports. The president agreed to do so. Kennedy helped pass several other measures important to Massachusetts' textile industry. He also sponsored bills that improved his state's conservation programs.

To the disappointment of liberal Democrats, Kennedy soft-pedaled the

John F. Kennedy at the 1952 Democratic National Convention in Chicago, Ill. Hank Walker/Time & Life Pictures/Getty Images

demagogic excesses of Senator Joseph R. McCarthy of Wisconsin, who in the early 1950s conducted witch-hunting campaigns against government workers accused of being communists. Kennedy's father liked McCarthy, contributed to his campaign, and even entertained him in the family's compound at Hyannis Port on Cape Cod in Massachusetts. Kennedy himself disapproved of McCarthy, but, as he once observed, "Half my people in Massachusetts look on McCarthy as a hero." Yet, on the Senate vote over condemnation of McCarthy's conduct (1954), Kennedy expected to vote against him. He prepared a speech explaining why, but he was absent on the day of the vote. Later, at a National Press Club Gridiron dinner, costumed reporters sang, "Where were you, John, where were you, John, when the Senate censured Joe?" Actually, John had been in a hospital, in critical condition after back surgery. For six months afterward he lay strapped to a board in his father's house in Palm Beach, Florida. While recuperating he worked on *Profiles in Courage* (1956), an account of eight great American political leaders who had defied popular opinion in matters of conscience. The book was awarded a Pulitzer Prize in

1957. Although Kennedy was credited as the book's author, it was later revealed that his assistant Theodore Sorensen had done much of the research and writing.

Kennedy's service on the Select Committee of the Senate to Investigate Improper Activities in Labor-Management Relations also attracted considerable attention during this period. John's younger brother Robert was chief legal counsel for this group. The two Kennedys were frequently in the public eye in 1959 as the committee investigated racketeering among top labor union officials. John sponsored a labor bill that did a great deal to eliminate criminal practices in unions.

Shortly after his election to the Senate, Kennedy met his future wife, Jacqueline Lee Bouvier, at a Washington, D.C., party. Jackie was the daughter of a Long Island family. At the time they met, she was a photographer and a pen-and-ink artist for a Washington, D.C., newspaper. They were married on Sept. 12, 1953. Their daughter, Caroline Bouvier Kennedy, was born on Nov. 27, 1957. Their son, John Fitzgerald Kennedy, Jr., was born on Nov. 25, 1960, 17 days after Kennedy was elected president of the United States.

Jacqueline Bouvier Kennedy tossing her bridal bouquet on the occasion of her marriage to Massachusetts Sen. John F. Kennedy, 1953. Library of Congress Prints and Photographs Division

THE 1960 PRESIDENTIAL ELECTION

Following the 1956 national election, Kennedy began an elaborate campaign for the 1960 Democratic presidential nomination. His popularity increased. In 1958 he was reelected to the Senate by a margin of some 874,000 votes, more than any other Massachusetts senator had ever received. His brother Robert managed John's senatorial campaign. In 1958 Teddy, the youngest of the Kennedy family, worked with Robert in managing John's campaign for the Democratic nomination.

In the early months of 1960, Kennedy entered and won seven primary elections across the nation. During his campaign for the nomination, Kennedy often began his speeches with this remark: "Thanks for not voting for me in 1956." That was the year he barely missed being nominated vice-president on the Democratic ticket. Senator Estes Kefauver of Tennessee, who won the vice-presidential nomination, and Adlai E. Stevenson, the presidential nominee, were defeated in the 1956 election. Had Kennedy been nominated and

Button from John F. Kennedy's 1960 U.S. presidential campaign.
Courtesy of Michael Levy

defeated with Stevenson, his chances for the presidency might have been lost. Instead, at the 1960 Democratic convention in Los Angeles, Kennedy received his party's nomination on the first ballot.

During the ensuing presidential campaign Kennedy and Vice-President Richard M. Nixon met in four nationally televised debates. It was generally conceded that these television appearances helped Kennedy more than Nixon.

In the election that November, Kennedy narrowly defeated Nixon. Although he and his vice-presidential running mate, Lyndon B. Johnson, got less than half of the more than 68 million votes cast, they won the electoral college vote. Many observers, then and since, believed vote fraud contributed to Kennedy's victory, especially in the critical state of Illinois, where Joseph Kennedy enlisted the help of the powerful Richard J. Daley, mayor of Chicago. Nixon had defended the Eisenhower record; Kennedy, whose slogan had been "Let's get this country moving again," had deplored unemployment, the sluggish economy, the so-called missile gap (a presumed Soviet superiority over the United States in the number of nuclear-armed missiles), and the new communist government in Cuba.

The Kennedy-Nixon Debates

On Sept. 26, 1960, a debate between the two major candidates for the presidency of the United States was presented on television for the first time. A total of four debates between John F. Kennedy and Richard M. Nixon were televised. The first debate, though, was the most influential and the most watched, reaching a then-record audience estimated to be about 70 million. That important political issues could be discussed by the candidates for the country's highest office and made effortlessly accessible to the nearly 90 percent of American homes that had televisions by 1960 demonstrated television's ability to play an important civic role in American life.

For all of the prestige that TV garnered from the broadcasts of the Kennedy-Nixon debates, however, controversy quickly surrounded them as well. Many argued that television was changing the political process and that

John F. Kennedy and Richard M. Nixon during one of their presidential debates in 1960. Paul Schutzer/Time & Life Pictures/Getty Images

how one looked and presented oneself on TV was more important than what one said. This seemed to be the case during the first debate. Younger, tanned, and dressed in a dark suit, Kennedy appeared to overshadow the more haggard, gray-suited Nixon, whose hastily applied makeup job scarcely covered his late-in-the-day stubble of facial hair. Informal surveys taken after the debate indicated that audiences who listened on the radio tended to think Nixon had won, while those who watched on TV claimed victory for Kennedy. Many also believed that Kennedy won the election because he won the first debate and that he won the first debate because he looked better on TV than his opponent. (It must be remembered, however, that the un-telegenic Nixon would go on to win two presidential elections.) Arguments about the impact of television on politics, of course, continue to be central to the political process to this day.

CHAPTER 3

The Presidency

Kennedy's administration lasted 1,037 days. From the onset he was concerned with foreign affairs. In his memorable inaugural address, he called upon Americans "to bear the burden of a long twilight struggle...against the common enemies of man: tyranny, poverty, disease, and war itself." He also urged his fellow citizens to "ask not what your country can do for you—ask what you can do for your country."

Kennedy proved to be an immensely popular president, at home and abroad. At times he seemed to be everywhere at once, encouraging better physical fitness, improving the morale of government workers, bringing brilliant advisers to the White House, and beautifying Washington, D.C. His wife joined him as an advocate for American

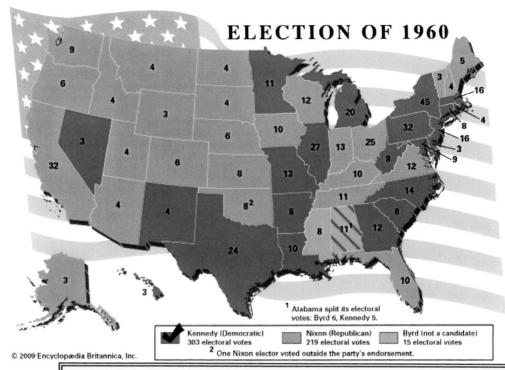

Results of the American presidential election, 1960. Encyclopædia Britannica, Inc.

Presidential Candidate	Political Party	Electoral Votes	Popular Votes
John F. Kennedy	Democratic	303	34,227,096
Richard Nixon	Republican	219	34,107,646
Harry F. Byrd	(not a candidate)	15	
Eric Hass	Socialist Labor		47,522
Rutherford L. Decker	Prohibition		46,203
Orval Faubus	National States' Rights		44,977
Farrell Dobbs	Socialist Workers		40,165
Charles L. Sullivan	Constitution		18,169

Sources: Electoral and popular vote totals based on data from the Office of the Clerk of the U.S. House of Representatives and *Congressional Quarterly's Guide to U.S. Elections*, 4th ed. (2001).

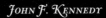

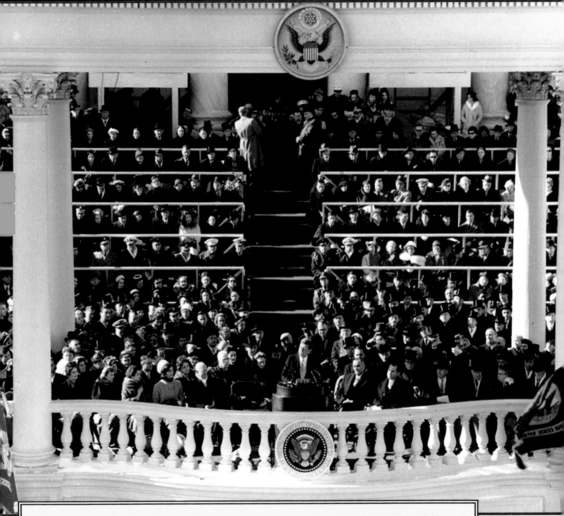

U.S. Pres. John F. Kennedy delivering his inaugural address, Washington, D.C., Jan. 20, 1961. CWO Donald Mingfield—U.S. Army Signal Corps/John F. Kennedy Presidential Library

culture. Their two young children, Caroline Bouvier and John Jr., were familiar throughout the country. The charm and optimism of the Kennedy family seemed contagious,

John F. Kennedy, 1961. AP

A young John F. Kennedy, Jr., pays a visit to the Oval Office. Universal Images Group/Getty Images

sparking the idealism of a generation for whom the Kennedy White House became, in journalist Theodore White's famous analogy, Camelot—the magical court of Arthurian legend, which was celebrated in a popular Broadway musical of the early 1960s.

First Lady Jacqueline Bouvier Kennedy

The glamorous and attractive wife of John F. Kennedy, Jacqueline Bouvier Kennedy, brought grace, style, and a flair for beauty to the White House, quickly becoming a celebrity in her own right. At 31 years of age when her husband took office, she was the youngest first lady in nearly 80 years, and she left a distinct mark on the job. During the 1960 election campaign she hired Letitia Baldrige, who was both politically savvy and astute on matters of etiquette, to assist her as social secretary. Through Baldrige, Jacqueline announced that she intended to make the White House a showcase for the country's most talented and accomplished individuals, and she invited musicians, actors, and intellectuals to the executive mansion.

The first lady's most enduring contribution was her work to restore the White House to its original elegance and to protect its holdings. She established the White House Historical Association, which was charged with educating the public and raising funds, and she wrote the foreword to the association's first edition of *The White House: An Historic Guide* (1962). To catalog the mansion's holdings, Jacqueline hired a curator from the Smithsonian Institution, a job that eventually became permanent. Congress, acting with the first lady's support, passed a law to encourage donations of valuable art and furniture and made White House furnishings of "artistic or historic importance" the "inalienable property" of the nation, thus prohibiting residents from disposing of them at will. After extensive refurbishing, Jacqueline hosted a tour of the White House that aired nationally on television in February 1962.

Jacqueline became one of history's most popular first ladies. During her travels with the president to Europe (1961) and Central and South America (1962), she won wide praise for her beauty, fashion sense, and facility with languages. Alluding to his wife's popularity during their tour of France in 1961, the president jokingly reintroduced himself to reporters as "the man who accompanied Jacqueline Kennedy to Paris." Parents named their daughters after Jacqueline, and women copied her bouffant

Jacqueline Bouvier Kennedy in 1961. Robert Knudsen— Official White House Photo/John F. Kennedy Presidential Library

hairstyle, pillbox hat, and flat-heeled pumps. In the aftermath of her husband's assassination in November 1963, the quiet dignity demonstrated by Jacqueline Kennedy elicited an outpouring of admiration and sympathy from Americans and from all over the world.

U.S. Pres. John F. Kennedy with First Lady Jacqueline Kennedy, 1961. Art Rickerby/Time & Life Pictures/Getty Images

PROBLEMS FACING THE NEW PRESIDENT

As Kennedy took office, Cold War tensions between communist and Western nations increased. Communist forces pushed into Laos and threatened South Vietnam. The new president pledged strong efforts to halt

U.S. Pres. John F. Kennedy in a televised press conference discussing the arrival of American military advisers in Vietnam, 1961. **National Archives/Getty Images**

the spread of communism. Toward this end, he created a Peace Corps of young Americans to work in underdeveloped countries.

After the Soviets successfully launched the first human into outer space in April 1961, Kennedy asked for a greatly increased budget for space research. This new phase of the Cold War was called the space race. The first United States manned space flight was in May.

Later in the spring of 1961 the Bay of Pigs near Havana, Cuba, was invaded by opponents of Cuba's communist premier, Fidel Castro. The rebels were defeated quickly. The

U.S. Pres. John F. Kennedy speaking about the U.S. space program at Rice University in Houston, Tex., Sept. 12, 1962. **Encyclopædia Britannica, Inc.**

invasion had been aided by the United States Central Intelligence Agency (CIA). Kennedy was criticized by some for having approved the CIA's support of the invasion. Others blamed him for the operation's failure.

Kennedy met with Premier Nikita Khrushchev of the Soviet Union in Vienna, Austria, in June to discuss another problem area—Berlin. The conference did not alter communist goals of limiting the influence of Western powers in the city and the region. In August, to halt the flow of refugees to the

A group of captured U.S.-backed Cuban exiles, known as Brigade 2506, being lined up by Fidel Castro's soldiers at the Bahía de Cochinos (Bay of Pigs), Cuba, following an unsuccessful invasion of the island, April 1961. **Three Lions/Hulton Archive/Getty Images**

West, Soviet and East German troops erected a wall of concrete and barbed wire that divided East and West Berlin. This barrier, known as the Berlin Wall, came to symbolize the Cold War's division of East from West Germany and of eastern from western Europe.

At home Kennedy won congressional approval of a number of his proposals, including greater Social Security benefits, a higher minimum wage, and aid to economically depressed areas in the country. The 23rd Amendment to the United States Constitution was ratified early in Kennedy's administration. It gave the residents of Washington, D.C., the right to vote in presidential elections.

In March 1961 Kennedy proposed an international economic development program for the United States and 22 Latin American countries. The charter for the program, called the Alliance for Progress, was ratified in August by the Organization of American States (OAS).

EVENTS OF 1962

In March 1962 Kennedy used his influence to get a steel-industry wage settlement generally regarded as noninflationary. Early in

The Peace Corps

The Peace Corps, a U.S. government agency of volunteers, grew out of a 1960 presidential campaign proposal by John F. Kennedy to find new ways of halting the spread of communism in underdeveloped countries. The first director of the Peace Corps was Kennedy's brother-in-law R. Sargent Shriver.

The Peace Corps Act of 1961 established the government-funded service as an agency in the U.S. Department of State. (When the independent agency ACTION was formed in 1971 to consolidate various volunteer programs, the Peace Corps was included. It became an independent agency in 1982.)

Pres. John F. Kennedy greeting Peace Corps volunteers at the White House, Aug. 28, 1961. Courtesy of the Peace Corps

The declared purpose of the Peace Corps is to promote the progress of other countries by providing them with skilled workers in the fields of education, agriculture, health, trade, technology, and community development. Peace Corps volunteers are assigned to specific projects on the basis of their ability, education, and experience. They serve overseas for two years after being trained in the local language, the technical requirements of the assigned job, and cross-cultural skills to help them adjust to a different society.

The Peace Corps grew from 750 volunteers serving 13 countries in 1961 to more than 15,000 volunteers in 52 countries in 1966. By 1989 budget cuts had reduced the number of volunteers to 5,100, but over the next two decades there were increases; by the Peace Corps's 50th anniversary in 2011, there were more than 8,500 volunteers serving in 77 countries.

April, however, several companies announced increases in their steel prices. Kennedy reacted strongly. He exerted unusual pressure by shifting government orders to rival steel manufacturers and by threatening lawsuits against the companies that were attempting to raise their prices. Within four days the price increases were canceled.

Kennedy's most important legislative success of 1962 was the passage of the Trade Expansion Act. It gave the president broad

(Left to right) *Robert F. Kennedy, Ted Kennedy, and Pres. John F. Kennedy,* c. *1962.* Hulton Archive/Archive Photos/ Getty Images

powers, including authority to cut or eliminate tariffs. The act was designed to help the United States compete or trade with the European Economic Community (EEC) on equal terms. A legislative loss, however, came when Kennedy's medical care project was defeated in Congress. Under this plan certain hospital expenses for most elderly persons would have been paid through the Social Security system.

In October 1962 Kennedy faced the most serious international crisis of his administration. Aerial photographs showed that Soviet missile bases were being built in Cuba. Declaring this buildup a threat to the nations of the Western Hemisphere, Kennedy warned that any attack by Cuba would be regarded as an attack by the Soviets and the United States would retaliate against the Soviet Union. He also imposed a quarantine on ships bringing offensive weapons to Cuba. Negotiations

President John F. Kennedy announcing the U.S. naval blockade of Cuba on Oct. 22, 1962. © **Archive Photos**

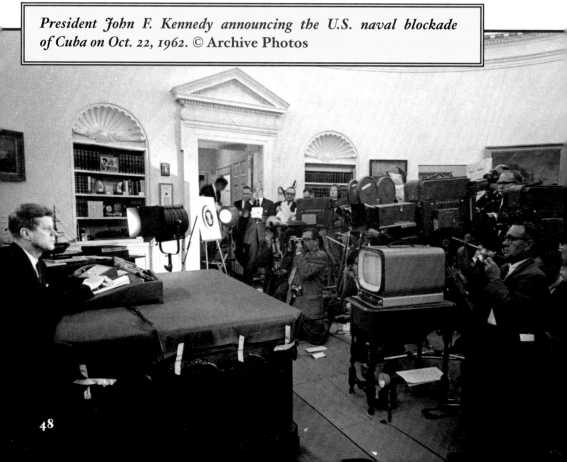

were carried on between the president and Khrushchev. By the end of November the missiles had been shipped back to the Soviet Union, the United States had lifted the quarantine, and the month-long crisis had abated.

KENNEDY'S FINAL ACCOMPLISHMENTS

In 1963 clashes between the police and demonstrating African Americans in Birmingham, Ala., and elsewhere, especially in the South, induced the president to stress civil rights legislation. Kennedy's new civil rights message included bills to ban discrimination in places of business, to speed up desegregation of public schools, and to end discrimination in the hiring of workers on federal construction projects.

In the international arena, a limited but promising achievement was realized when an agreement to set up a Teletype link between Kennedy and Khrushchev was signed in

American civil rights leaders meeting with government officials at the White House on the day of the March on Washington, Aug. 28, 1963. Cecil Stoughton—Official White House Photo/John F. Kennedy Presidential Library

June 1963. This newly opened avenue of communication was intended as a precaution against war by accident or miscalculation.

The president also paid increasing attention to strengthening the North Atlantic Treaty Organization (NATO). Visiting Europe early in the summer of 1963, he conferred with government leaders in West Germany, Italy, and the United Kingdom. In West Germany,

U.S. Pres. John F. Kennedy signing the Nuclear Test-Ban Treaty, Oct. 7, 1963. **National Archives and Records Administration**

the president pledged that United States military forces would remain on the European continent. Kennedy also visited Ireland, from which his great-grandparents had emigrated to the United States.

Several months later the Nuclear Test-Ban Treaty was signed by representatives of the United States, the Soviet Union, and the United Kingdom. The agreement banned all tests of nuclear weapons except those conducted underground, and signatory nations could withdraw after 90 days' notice. Kennedy called the treaty a "victory for mankind."

CHAPTER 4

Assassination

President Kennedy believed that his Republican opponent in 1964 would be Senator Barry Goldwater of Arizona. He was convinced that he could bury Goldwater under an avalanche of votes, thus receiving a mandate for major legislative reforms. One obstacle to his plan was a feud in Vice-President Johnson's home state of Texas between Governor John B. Connally, Jr., and Senator Ralph Yarborough, both Democrats. To present a show of unity, the president decided to tour the state with both men in November 1963. Kennedy's wife, Vice-President Johnson, and Mrs. Johnson accompanied him on the Texas trip.

Kennedy had been warned that Texas might be hostile. In Dallas, only a month earlier, Adlai Stevenson, United States ambassador to the United Nations, had been spat upon and struck with a picketer's placard. In San Antonio, Houston, and Fort Worth, however, the crowds were friendly and obviously delighted with the charming young Jacqueline Kennedy.

THE SHOOTING IN DALLAS

A large and enthusiastic crowd greeted the presidential party when it arrived at the Dallas airport on the morning of November 22. Along the route of the motorcade into downtown Dallas the people stood 10 to 12 deep, applauding warmly. Next to the president in a big open limousine sat his wife. In front of them, on jump seats, were John B. Connally, the governor of Texas, and his wife, Nellie. The third car in the procession carried Vice-President and Mrs. Johnson. As the cars approached an underpass, Mrs. Connally turned around and said, "You can't say Dallas doesn't love you, Mr. President."

At that moment three shots rang out. The president, shot through the throat and head, slumped over into his wife's lap. The second bullet hit Governor Connally, piercing his back, chest, wrist, and thigh. A reporter,

U.S. Pres. John F. Kennedy and first lady Jacqueline Kennedy shortly before the president was assassinated in Dallas, Nov. 22, 1963. Texas governor John B. Connally and his wife, Nellie, are seated in front of the Kennedys. © Everett Collection/SuperStock

glancing up, saw a rifle slowly disappear into a sixth-floor corner window of the Texas School Book Depository, a warehouse overlooking the highway. It was 12:30 PM in Dallas.

President Kennedy died in Parkland Memorial Hospital without regaining consciousness. The time of death was set at 1:00 PM. Governor Connally recovered from his multiple wounds.

Six minutes after the shooting, a description of a man seen leaving the textbook warehouse went out over the police radio. At 1:18 PM patrolman J.D. Tippit stopped and questioned a man who answered the description. The man shot the patrolman dead. At 1:35 PM Dallas police captured Lee Harvey Oswald in a motion-picture theater, where he had hidden after allegedly killing Officer Tippit.

Although a mass of circumstantial evidence, including ballistics tests, pointed to Oswald as the slayer of President Kennedy, the 24-year-old professed Marxist and Castro sympathizer never came to trial. On Sunday, November 24, as he was being led across the basement of the City Hall for transfer to another prison, Jack Ruby (born Rubenstein), a Dallas nightclub owner, broke through a cordon of police and shot Oswald. The murder was committed in full view of television cameras as millions watched.

THE RETURN TO WASHINGTON

The casket bearing Kennedy's body was removed to the presidential airplane, Air Force One, where Lyndon B. Johnson took the oath of office as president of the United States. Only 98 minutes had elapsed since Kennedy's death.

All that long afternoon and into the early morning of the next day, Mrs. Kennedy refused to leave her husband's body. Close by her side at all times after her return to Washington, D.C., was her husband's brother and closest adviser, Attorney General Robert F. Kennedy. Mrs. Kennedy carefully directed the details of the funeral, consulting with historians as

Jacqueline Kennedy and Lady Bird Johnson standing by U.S. Pres. Lyndon B. Johnson as he takes the oath of office aboard Air Force One after the assassination of John F. Kennedy, Nov. 22, 1963. Lyndon B. Johnson Library Photo

to the traditional burial procedures for other presidents who had died in office.

BURIAL AT ARLINGTON

The body lay in repose for a day in the East Room of the White House. On November

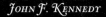

Pres. John F. Kennedy's body being carried by pallbearers into the U.S. Capitol rotunda, Nov. 24, 1963. **Encyclopædia Britannica, Inc.**

24, in a solemn procession to the slow beat of muffled drums, the casket was removed to the rotunda of the Capitol and placed on the catafalque that had borne President Abraham Lincoln's casket.

The following day the funeral procession moved from the Capitol to the White House and then to St. Matthew's Cathedral. There Richard Cardinal Cushing, Roman Catholic archbishop of Boston, celebrated Low Mass. From the White House to the cathedral,

The body of Pres. John F. Kennedy lying in state in the U.S. Capitol rotunda, Nov. 24, 1963. Encyclopædia Britannica, Inc.

Mrs. Kennedy walked in the procession between her husband's brothers, Robert and Edward. In a scene unduplicated in history, 220 foreign leaders followed them.

Burial was at Arlington National Cemetery, on a hillside overlooking the Potomac River and the city of Washington. At the conclusion of the service, Mrs. Kennedy lighted an eternal flame at the grave.

Two Kennedy infants were later reburied on either side of their father. They were

Pres. John F. Kennedy's funeral procession on its way to Arlington National Cemetery, Nov. 25, 1963. Encyclopædia Britannica, Inc.

At the funeral of Pres. John F. Kennedy, brothers Edward (left) and Robert stand to either side of Jacqueline Kennedy. Caroline is seen to the left of her mother, and John Jr. salutes his father. It was John Jr.'s third birthday. Popperfoto/Getty Images

Patrick Bouvier and an unnamed daughter who was stillborn in 1956.

In his proclamation declaring Nov. 25, 1963, a National Day of Mourning for John Kennedy, President Johnson paid this tribute to the slain president, quoting in conclusion from Kennedy's inaugural address of January 1960: "As he did not shrink from his responsibilities, but welcomed them, so he would not have us shrink from carrying on his work beyond this hour of national tragedy. He said it himself: 'The energy, the faith, the devotion which we bring to this endeavor will light our country and all who serve it—and the glow from that fire can truly light the world.'"

On June 8, 1968, the Kennedy family and a host of other mourners again gathered at the Kennedy grave site—this time for the burial of Robert F. Kennedy. The president's brother, who had become a United States senator, was shot on June 5 in Los Angeles, Calif., while campaigning for the Democratic presidential nomination. He died on June 6. Sirhan Bishara Sirhan, a Jordanian immigrant who was seized at the scene of the shooting, was eventually indicted for the murder.

For the second time President Johnson declared a day of mourning for a Kennedy. Many of the same Americans who honored Robert

Kennedy's memory on June 9, 1968, were sadly reminded of an earlier day of mourning.

THE WARREN COMMISSION

On Nov. 29, 1963, President Johnson created the President's Commission on the Assassination of President John F. Kennedy to investigate and report on the facts relating to the tragedy. It functioned neither as a court nor as a prosecutor. The chief justice of the Supreme Court, Earl Warren, was appointed chairman.

Other members of the bipartisan commission were Senators Richard B. Russell of Georgia and John Sherman Cooper of Kentucky, Representatives Hale Boggs of Louisiana and Gerald R. Ford of Michigan, Allen W. Dulles, and John J. McCloy. J. Lee Rankin was the general counsel. The report was published nearly a year later, on Sept. 24, 1964.

Because Oswald was unable to stand trial and defend himself, and in fairness to him and his family, the commission requested Walter E. Craig, president of the American Bar Association, to participate in the investigation and to advise the commission whether the proceedings conformed to the basic principles of United States justice.

The commission found that the shots that killed President Kennedy and wounded Governor Connally were fired by Lee Harvey Oswald. There was no evidence at that time that either Oswald or Jack Ruby was part of any conspiracy, domestic or foreign, to assassinate President Kennedy. No direct or indirect relationship between Oswald and Ruby had been uncovered. On the basis of the evidence before it, the commission concluded that Oswald acted alone. Despite the findings of the commission, conspiracy theories persisted for decades.

The commission criticized both the Secret Service and the Federal Bureau of Investigation (FBI). Some of the advance preparations and

Lee Harvey Oswald holding a Russian newspaper and a rifle; the Warren Commission concluded that the rifle was used to assassinate U.S. Pres. John F. Kennedy. **Donald Uhrbrock/Time & Life Pictures/Getty Images**

security measures in Dallas made by the Secret Service were found to have been deficient. In addition, though the FBI had obtained considerable information about Oswald, it had no official responsibility to refer this information to the Secret Service. "A more carefully coordinated treatment of the Oswald case by the FBI might well have resulted in bringing Oswald's activities to the attention of the Secret Service," the report stated.

The commission made suggestions for improved protective measures of the Secret Service and better liaison with the FBI, the Department of State, and other federal agencies. Other recommendations were:

- That a committee of Cabinet members, or the National Security Council, should review and oversee the protective activities of the Secret Service and other agencies that help safeguard the president.
- That Congress adopt legislation that would make the assassination of the president and vice-president a federal crime.
- That the representatives of the bar, law enforcement associations, and the news media establish ethical standards concerning the collection

and presentation of information to the public so that there will be no interference with pending criminal investigations, court proceedings, or the right of individuals to a fair trial.

The Enduring Kennedy Mystique

John F. Kennedy was dead, but the Kennedy mystique was still alive. Both Robert and Ted ran for president (in 1968 and 1980, respectively). After Robert was assassinated on the campaign trail in 1968, tragedy became nearly synonymous with the Kennedys.

Upon leaving the White House, Jacqueline Kennedy and her two children moved to a home in the Georgetown section of Washington. Continuing crowds of the worshipful and curious made peace there impossible, however, and in the summer of 1964 she moved to New York City. Pursuit continued until October 20, 1968, when she married Aristotle Onassis, a wealthy Greek shipping magnate. The Associated Press said that the marriage "broke the spell of almost complete adulation of a woman who had become virtually a legend in her own time." Widowed by Onassis, the former first lady returned to the public eye in the mid-1970s as a high-profile book editor, and she remained among the most admired women in the United States until her death in 1994. As an adult, daughter Caroline was protective of her own privacy, but John Jr. — a lawyer like his sister and debonair and handsome like his father—was much more of a public figure. Long remembered as "John-John," the three-year-old who stoically saluted his father's casket during live television coverage of the funeral procession, John Jr. became the founder and editor-in-chief of the political magazine *George* in the mid-1990s. In 1999, when John Jr., his wife, and his sister-in-law died in the crash of the private plane he was piloting, the event was the focus of an international media watch that further proved the immortality of the Kennedy mystique. It was yet another chapter in the family's "curse" of tragedy.

Portrait of Pres. John F. Kennedy by Aaron Shikler, 1970. Encyclopædia Britannica, Inc.

CONCLUSION

Although John F. Kennedy's time in the White House lasted less than three years, the influence of his presidency on the United States was profound and long-lasting. His election infused the country with new vigor. On the campaign trail he had promised to "get America moving again," and once in office, he appointed a Cabinet and staff who shared his belief that the United States could be doing far more to prove its technological and moral superiority over the Soviet Union, win the "hearts and minds" of people in developing countries, and accelerate social progress at home.

On all of these fronts, Kennedy had notable success or paved the way for significant progress in the future. Alarmed by the impact of the Soviet space program on world opinion, he committed the United States to landing a man on the Moon by the end of the decade — a goal that was realized with the Apollo 11 spaceflight in July 1969. Kennedy was also a vocal critic of communism, and his proposals for the Peace Corps and the Alliance for Progress were part of his efforts to actively promote the expansion of democracy abroad. On the home front he submitted a sweeping civil rights bill to Congress on June 19, 1963. Although this measure initially received little support in Congress, a stronger version was eventually passed with the urging of Kennedy's successor, Lyndon B. Johnson, who signed the bill into law on July 2, 1964.

Glossary

ballistics Science of the motion of projectiles in flight.

bipartisan Marked by or involving cooperation, agreement, and compromise between two major political parties.

catafalque Ornamental structure sometimes used in funerals for the lying in state of the body.

censure Judgment involving condemnation; an official reprimand.

compound Fenced or walled-in area containing a group of buildings (especially residences).

debonair Having very polished and worldly manners; suave.

demagogic Aiming to gain personal or partisan advantage by arousing or appealing to popular passions or prejudices, especially by making deceptive or extravagant claims, promises, or charges.

endowment Permanent provision of financial support.

inaugurate Induct into an office with suitable ceremonies.

Low Mass As distinguished from Mass, which is a sequence of prayers and ceremonies in a Catholic church commemorating Jesus Christ, Low Mass is recited without singing by the celebrant, without a deacon or choir, and without the use of incense. (In Catholicism, a deacon is an official of the church whose rank is below that of a priest.)

magnate Person of rank, power, or influence in a particular field.

mandate Support given by voters to an elected representative by virtue of their votes cast in an election; the more plentiful the votes, the clearer the mandate.

marquess European title of nobility ranking in modern times immediately below a duke and above a count or earl.

noninflationary Not inflationary, that is, not contributing to a general increase in prices.

pallbearer One who helps to carry the coffin at a funeral.

placard Poster affixed to a stick.

premier Prime minister.

quarantine State of enforced isolation.

rotunda Large round room.

signatory Signer with another or others, especially a government bound with others by a signed convention.

soft-pedal Play something down; obscure or muffle a fact or consideration.

tariff Tax placed on products because they go from one nation to another (also known as duty and customs). Although all tariffs raise money for the governments that impose them, tariffs may also be used to protect domestic industries.

Teletype Trademark for a kind of typewriter called a teleprinter that was used to send typed messages to one or more recipients by means of an electrical connection.

ward Election district within a city.

witch hunt The searching out and deliberate harassment of those (such as political opponents) with unpopular views.

For More Information

American Historical Association (AHA)
400 A Street SE
Washington, DC 20003
(202) 544-2422
Web site: http://www.historians.org
The AHA serves as a leader and advocate for professionals, researchers, and students in the field of history as it upholds academic and professional standards.

John Fitzgerald Kennedy National Historic Site
83 Beals Street
Brookline, MA 02446
(617) 566-7937
Web site: www.nps.gov/jofi
The birthplace of the 35th U.S. president, the John F. Kennedy National Historic Site has been restored to its 1917 appearance (the year of Kennedy's

birth) and is open to the public for
tours and events.

John F. Kennedy Presidential Library
    and Museum
Columbia Point
Boston, MA 02125
(866) JFK-1960
Web site: http://www.jfklibrary.org
With an extensive collection of both arti-
    facts and papers documenting the life,
    career, and times of John F. Kennedy, the
    John F. Kennedy Presidential Library
    and Museum preserves the legacy of the
    nation's 35th president and encourages
    public interest in his many contributions.

Miller Center
2201 Old Ivy Road
Charlottesville, VA 22904
(434) 924-7236
Web site: http://millercenter.org
The Miller Center at the University of
    Virginia furthers understanding of
    the presidency, political history, and
    policy through its various research
    initiatives, programs, events, and
    fellowship opportunities.

Sixth Floor Museum at Dealey Plaza
411 Elm Street
Dallas, TX 75202
(214) 747-6660
Web site: http://www.jfk.org
Located in the warehouse once known as
the Texas School Book Depository, the
exhibits at the Sixth Floor Museum at
Dealey Plaza chronicle both the life and
death of John F. Kennedy and examine
the impact his assassination had on the
U.S. and the world.

WEB SITES

Due to the changing nature of Internet links,
Rosen Educational Services has developed an
online list of Web sites related to the subject of
this book. This site is updated regularly. Please
use this link to access the list:

http://www.rosenlinks.com/pppl/jfk

For Further Reading

Anzovin, Steven, and others, eds. *Facts About the Presidents: A Compilation of Biographical and Historical Information*, 7th ed. (Wilson, 2001).

Ashby, Ruth. *John & Jacqueline Kennedy* (World Almanac Library, 2005).

Heiligman, Deborah. *High Hopes: A Photobiography of John F. Kennedy* (National Geographic, 2003).

Hodge, Marie. *John F. Kennedy: Voice of Hope* (Sterling, 2007). Mara, Wil. *John F. Kennedy* (Marshall Cavendish Benchmark, 2010).

Matthews, Christopher. *Kennedy & Nixon: The Rivalry That Shaped Postwar America* (Simon & Schuster, 1996).

May, E.R., and Zelikow, P.D., eds. *The Kennedy Tapes: Inside the White House During the Cuban Missile Crisis* (Belknap, 2000).

Raatma, Lucia. *John F. Kennedy* (Compass Point Books, 2002).

Sommer, Shelley. *John F. Kennedy: His Life and Legacy* (HarperCollins, 2005). Spencer, Lauren. *The Assassination of John F. Kennedy* (Rosen, 2002).

Index